W9-AVH-546

you'll know you're a *nurse* when...

Sigma Theta Tau International
Honor Society of Nursing®

Sigma Theta Tau International

Sigma Theta Tau International
550 West North Street
Indianapolis, IN 46202

To order additional books, buy in bulk, or order for corporate use, contact Nursing Knowledge International at 888.NKI.4YOU (888.654.4968/US and Canada) or +1.317.634.8171.

To request a review copy for course adoption, e-mail solutions@nursingknowledge.org or call 888.NKI.4YOU (888.654.4968/US and Canada) or +1.317.917.4983.

To request author information, or for speaker or other media requests, contact Rachael McLaughlin at 888.634.7575 (US and Canada) or +1.317.634.8171.

ISBN-13: 978-1-930538-93-1

Printed in the United States of America
Printing and Binding by Edwards Brothers, Inc.

    Library of Congress Cataloging-in-Publication Data
You'll know you're a nurse when--.
    p. cm.
 ISBN 978-1-930538-93-1
1. Nursing--Vocational guidance--Humor. I. Sigma Theta Tau
International.
 RT82.Y68 2010
 610.7306'9--dc22
                    2009035803

First Printing, 2009

Publisher: Renee Wilmeth
Acquisitions Editor: Cynthia Saver, RN, MS
Development Editor: Carla Hall
Copy Editor: Jacqueline Tiery

Cover Design by: Rebecca Harmon
Interior Design and Page Composition by: Rebecca Harmon
Editorial Coordinator: Paula Jeffers

Table of Contents

Foreword

The art and science of nursing is something so profound and complex that it is often difficult to put into words. Any standard definition, even a comprehensive and well-thought out one, falls short of conveying the depth and breadth of nursing care, not to mention the day-to-day experience and the psyche of the average nurse. Some things can only be conveyed in an anecdotal manner. That's where *You'll Know You're a Nurse When . . .* comes in.

The quotes and vignettes contained herein will make you laugh and probably tear up. You'll nod your head in quiet understanding. You'll whisper a silent "yes" as you discover that another nurse has put into words something you have felt, experienced, known on some level—and perhaps didn't realize how universal it was in the world of nursing. You'll occasionally get goose bumps as you share in another nurse's thoughts and feelings.

You'll Know You're a Nurse When . . . celebrates nursing in all its glory, sacredness, value, and humor. It will make you feel proud (or even prouder) to be a nurse, but with a better understanding of what's so great about it. It gives voice and context to the nursing experience in a lighthearted and easy to read way, and that is empowering and inspiring.

Read it often, share it with nursing and non-nursing colleagues, and reflect on what being a nurse means to you and why you keep on doing what you do so well.

—*Donna Wilk Cardillo, RN, MA*
Keynote Speaker and Author, A Daybook for Beginning Nurses,
The ULTIMATE Career Guide for Nurses, *and* Your 1st Year as a Nurse
"Dear Donna" columnist for Nursing Spectrum *and* Nurseweek magazines

1

inspiration/
philosophy

"…You hold a dying baby and sing a lullaby, you thank a wounded warrior for a job well done, you rejoice with a family over a life well lived, and you know that you have made a difference."

–Debra Craig
San Diego, California

"…You can instantly put aside all your problems, frustrations (personal or work-related), and ills and give 100% of your strength, compassion, and focus to your patient. There's nothing like a nurse's heart."

–Geralde Pierre
North Hollywood, California

"…You're called upon to provide care and compassion to a dying man for the last four weeks of his life; his family relies on you for your knowledge and expertise. He is your father."

–Bobbie Goltz, RN, MSN
Fort Wayne, Indiana

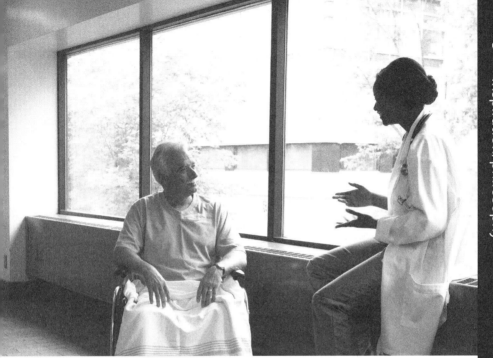

"…You see every person and situation
in terms of an opportunity for health
promotion and don't hesitate to act on it."

–Jeanmarie Wong
San Clemente, California

"…You save a life, ease a client's pain, show that someone cares, or make a change in the world no matter how small and have that special warm inner feeling that only a nurse can feel."

–*Sheila M. Keller, RN, MSN*
Sicklerville, New Jersey

"...Your major goal in life is to touch as many souls as you can in your lifetime, unconditionally, in a loving, healing, caring, and compassionate way."

–Michael D. Arena, RN, BSN
Rochester, New York

"...You view the world through the eyes of a critical thinker and reflect on how you can restore homeostasis and make the world whole."

–Wendy Schiffman, RN
Mission Viejo, California

"…Caring for people and promoting optimal health and wellness transcends the work environment or schedule and permeates all aspects of life and all relationships and interactions."

–Martha Smith, MSN, RN
Marceline, Missouri

"…After 25 plus years as a nurse—and now an educator of nurses—you wake up each day with the same passion you have for nursing that you did long ago."

–Gina Robinson
Plantation, Florida

"…You find comfort in comforting."

–Janice Jones, RN, PhD, CNS
East Aurora, New York

How can I forget that day? It was when I went to Kashmir, Pakistan, in 2004 to help people suffering from the after effects of a tremendous earthquake. I met one client whom we were told was 135 years old. When I talked to him, I came to know that he had strong willpower, though he had lost everything in the earthquake—even his family—but he was thankful to God. His resilience and strong willpower taught me the lesson that we should always be thankful to God. From that day until now, I live my every moment happily. Sometimes patients and clients teach us things that remain in our memory forever. Therefore, we should not turn a deaf ear to anyone's suggestion or advice.

–Zehra Parvani, RN, BSN
Karachi, Pakistan

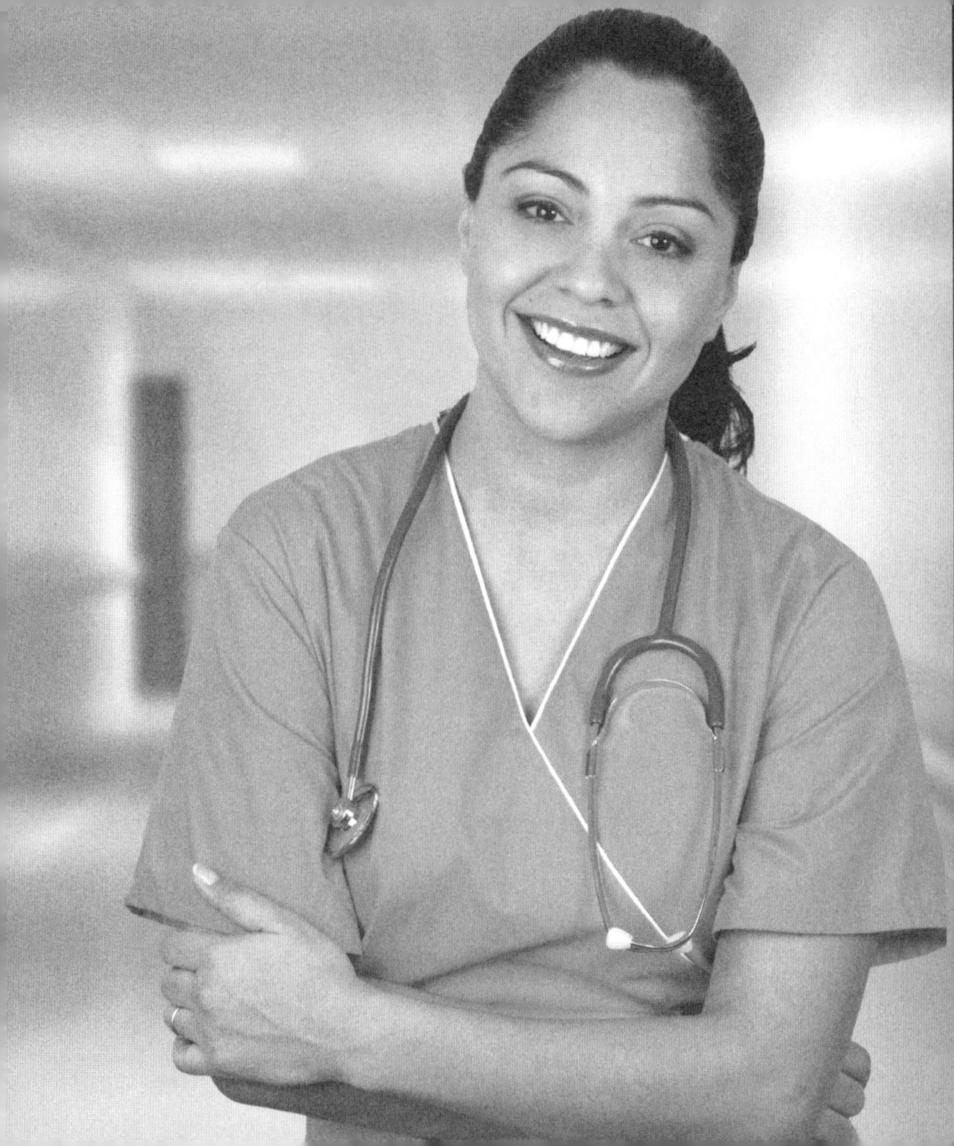

11 inspiration/philosophy

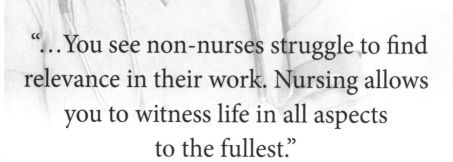

"…You see non-nurses struggle to find relevance in their work. Nursing allows you to witness life in all aspects to the fullest."

–Doris Ugarriza, PhD
Miami Beach, Florida

"…Your heart burns with love and pride that you have become a member of a profession that accepts the gift and challenge of caring for people in need."

–Rebecca Carron, MS, RN, NP-C
Centennial, Wyoming

"…You don't limit your knowledge to your work but spread it among family and friends, you believe that providing care should not be money driven, and you thrive to learn something new for your personal and professional growth."

–Charanpreet Walia
Laguna Niguel, California

"…You look eye-to-eye with disease and see only the woman, man, or child."

–RN-BSN leadership class, Walsh University
North Canton, Ohio
Submitted by Sherrie Underwood, RN, MSN, CNS,

"…You look across the patient's bed at a co-worker, smile, and know you both just understood and wordlessly 'spoke' the same language."

–Emily Vorwerk, BSN
Sylvania, Ohio

"…A former student tells a colleague what an impact you had on her becoming a knowledgeable and caring nurse—10 years after you've retired."

–Adriene K. Villotti, RN, BSN, MA
Mascoutah, Illinois

"…A visit to the Vietnam Women's Memorial evokes emotion every nurse has felt at some point in her or his practice, and that only other nurses understand."

–Ann Gabel, MSN, RN, BC
Leavenworth, Kansas

"…You've taught a novice nurse through sharing the experiences and knowledge of your career, and it enriched her practice."

–Connie Hatley, RN, BS
Tulsa, Oklahoma

In 1983, I was in my early 20s, and 26 weeks pregnant with my first child. I worked in the newborn intensive care unit in a hospital in the Bronx, New York. I was beyond novice, but certainly not an expert in the field—a field which was in its infancy in the early 1980s.

I was assigned two ventilator dependant premature infants, otherwise referred to as two barely viable preemies on vents. In those days, there were plenty of preemies with do not resuscitate (DNR) signs hanging over their heads, like little death warrants just waiting for that perfect moment. One of my *little chickens*, as I would call them, was particularly fragile. Several brain bleeds, necrotic intestines, all criteria for a poor outcome should she survive. Her parents were not at the bedside, as they were unable to stay at the hospital for more than brief visits since they had other young children at home.

I had just finished the vital signs and began to chart, when the ominous sounds of the monitor began alarming with the slowing down of the heart rate. All of the rote skills kicked in: Reposition, listen for breath sounds, suction. Nothing worked. As this was a DNR there was no code to call, no parents at the bedside, no residents, or for that matter, no other nurses. I was alone in the room with a dying baby, the same age as the life I carried inside. Despite the no code, I still called my nurse manager who was assisting with a procedure, and the resident—who did not respond to my beeper page. Again, I called the resident, who finally answered, and I explained the plight. "Well, did you get the time of death?" "Of course," I responded. "Well, I'll be there as soon as I can."

Finally, after all that could be done was done, I looked down at this little angel and felt a terrible sadness. When did a human life become so clinical, so abstract? I would not let this infant die without some sense of human dignity. The protocol for an infant who expired was clear and simple; there were tasks the nurses did, and there were tasks the residents did. After completing my nursing tasks and still waiting for the resident, I looked down at this cold little body and said to myself "no more." I cut the endotracheal tube, cut and tied the arterial line—tasks assigned to the residents—and I wrapped this tiny little being in a baby blanket, put a hat on her, and sat in the rocking chair. I said a prayer, hummed baby lullabies, and I waited.

That was my last day in the unit until I had my son. It all became just too sad, too close to home. I was only 24, but I know I learned an important life lesson that day, both as a human being and as a nurse.

–Mary McDermott, RN, BSN, CCM
Sparta, New Jersey

"…A student or patient contacts you several years later and thanks you for helping them when they needed it most."

–Anne Bateman, EdD, PMH-APRN, BC
Brewster, Massachusetts

"…You end the day with an empty stomach and full bladder but don't care because you had the chance to make a difference in the lives of those in your care. Your day was a good one!"

–Carma Hanson
Grand Links, North Dakota

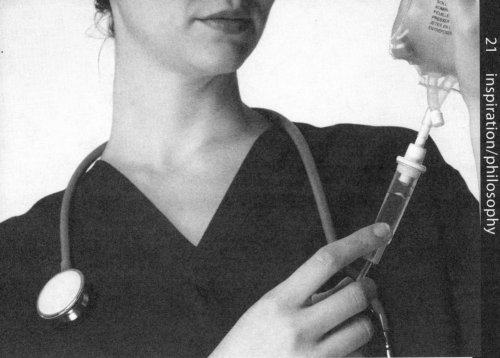

"…You realize that assisting others to become empowered is one of your greatest contributions."

–*Cathy Leahy*
Cincinnati, Ohio

To those considering nursing as a career, I say first and foremost you must have a servant heart. Nursing is the profession for those who truly love serving others without regard to socioeconomic status, culture, age, etc., and who expect nothing extrinsic in return. A nurse must be a true patient advocate, one who doesn't just "talk the talk" but who actually "walks the walk." Wherever a nurse serves, it is "holy ground." From assisting with the birth of a precious newborn to holding the cold, scared hand of one who is dying, it is a blessing and a privilege to be invited to share these extremely personal experiences with patients. Be ready to make a positive difference in the lives of those you touch.

–Jeanie Burt, MSN, MA, RN, CNE
Searcy, Arkansas

"…You are passionate about the well-being of other people and using professional nursing skills while delivering the more human side of health care called 'the nurse's touch.'"

–Michael Afienza
Lakewood, California

"…You feel an unending glow in your heart when you touch the souls of those who need you the most; your heart feels the warmth of your smile."

–Josephine DeVito, PhD, RN
Middletown, New Jersey

"…Your heart realizes death is a part of life, and there is such a thing as a good death."

–Joanne Sickler, RN, MSN
Charlotte Amalie, United States Virgin Islands

2

self-awareness

you'll know you're a nurse when ...

"...Everyone comes to you for all the questions about their health, when you talk about medical topics that no one would ever think about randomly, and when flexibility becomes the code that you live by."

–Mary Aguilar
Carson, California

"…You begin to have a hero complex, have altered sleep patterns, and become a hypochondriac. We all truly believe we can save the world, one person at a time."

–Valerie Puruganan
Pasadena, California

"…You feel confident in your knowledge and your skills."

–Julie Sult
Long Beach, California

"…You are teaching life skills and problem-solving to your child, partner, etc., and you realize you are talking about the nursing process."

–Robin Hertel, BSN, CMS, RN
Hays, Kansas

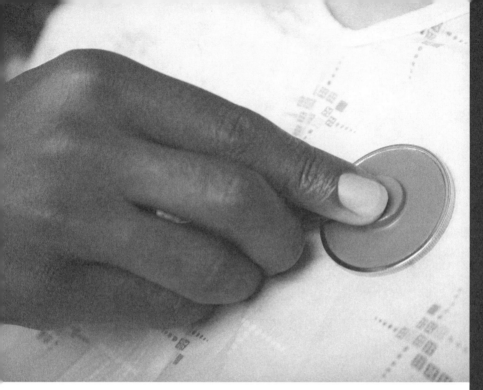

"…You realize that the little things you do can improve someone's quality of life."

–*Maria Satre, MSN, RN*
Hilliard, Ohio

"…You've worked 40-plus years in the profession and, when you look back, it seems like so much less. It was so much fun, and it all went too fast, but you'd do it all over again!"

–Wendy Stevens, RN, BSN, (Ret)
Port Townsend, Washington

"…You come to an international conference alone and meet up with another nurse you know from your past and share stories that make you laugh."

–Dianne Brown, RN, BSN, MN
Manitou, Manitoba, Canada

"…You start to make money, when you get your NCLEX results from the board of registered nursing, when you receive your first paycheck and splurge."

–Joel Delfin
Cavason, California

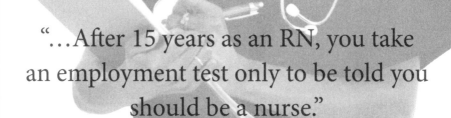

"…After 15 years as an RN, you take an employment test only to be told you should be a nurse."

–*Mary Stahl, RN, MSN*
Vicksburg, Michigan

"…You continue 'working' after retirement; retirement means saying 'no' once in a while.

–Adele D.S. Mitchell, RN, BSN, MSN, CNS
Kaneohe, Hawaii

"…You have your first out-of-body experience! That new grad comes to orientation on your unit and suddenly you are explaining how your 'brain' works, what to tell Dr. 'X' when you phone patient conditions, how to pass meds to a patient on time, etc. It was a pivotal moment for me . . . I made it (and didn't realize how much I knew)!"

–Colleen Kelley, MSN, RN
South Bend, Indiana

"…You constantly reflect about the things you could do to improve the care you deliver to your patients."

–Rebecca A. Gatesman, MSN, FNP
West Jordan, Utah

"…Upon earning your nurse practicitioner (NP) certification, family and friends say, 'You should've been a doctor,' and you respond, 'I don't want to be a doctor—I'm a nurse because nursing is my passion!'"

–Betty B. Small, BSN, RN, MSN, ANP-C
Portland, Maine

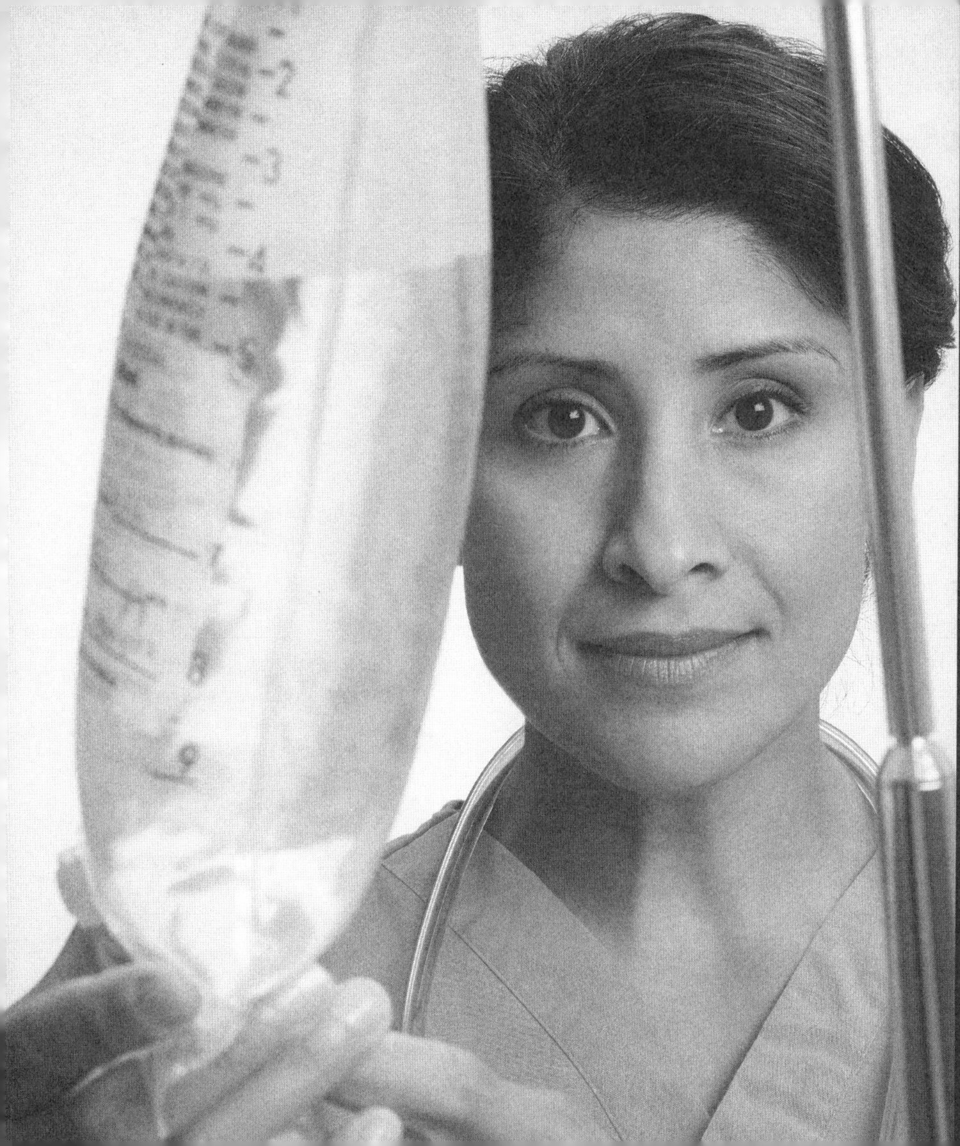

3

those dreaded
bodily functions

"…A post-op patient passes loud gas, and you say, 'that's music to my ears.'"

–Celine Fernandes
Yucaipa, California

"…Urine output is more valuable to you than gold bullion."

–Karyn Skiathitis, RN, BSN
Los Angeles, California

"…No matter what the subject matter, your appetite is not affected, even when others' are!"

–Shannon Steele, BSN
Little Rock, Arkansas

"…You gauge how busy your shift was by how many times you were able to use the bathroom."

–Ken Schmidt, RN, MSN, BC
Fairborn, Ohio

"…You heroically smile and don't run away from your elderly patient who shyly shows his appreciation by presenting you with a handful of stool."

–Raquel Gabriel-Bennewitz, MS, MBA, RN
Palos Park, Illinois

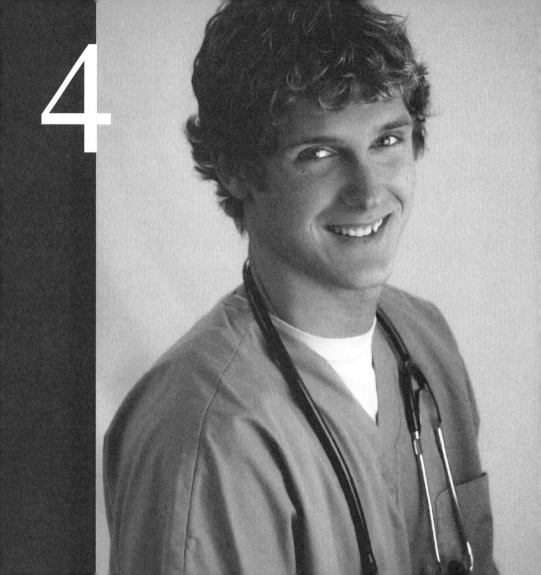

4

off-duty

"…Your glove compartment in your car has a pocket mask and non-latex gloves, and your purse has Band-Aids, clamps, mini-flashlight, Tylenol, tweezers, and Benadryl."

–Joan Kirschner
Los Angeles, California

"…You walk up to a perfect stranger in New York City and tell the mom to cut up that hot dog in small pieces before she gives it to her 1-year-old."

–Deborah Harris-Cobbinah, MSN, NP, CNS, BC
Bronx, New York

"…You replay your entire shift in your mind on the way home to make sure you didn't forget anything."

–Diane Tilkemeier, RN, MSN
Cumberland, Rhode Island

"…When you're working the night shift, you drink wine in the morning and coffee at night."

–Kathy Maddox, RN
Dumfries, Virginia

"… You're doing your laundry and think to yourself, 'are these blue scrubs all I wore last week?'"

–Melissa Erkel, RN, BSN
Presto, Pennsylvania

"…You open the refrigerator door and notice that the already opened milk jug has been dated and timed and has your initials on it."

–Kris Haws, RN, SRNA
Pawtucket, Rhode Island

"…You drive past the fast-food window to 'prepare' dinner for your family because you stayed with your patient until his or her family arrived."

–Linda Cicconi, RN, BSN, CNOR
Pittsburgh, Pennsylvania

"…You watch 'ER' to point out the mistakes."

–Colleen Baker, RN, BSN
Lebanon, New Hampshire

"...You quickly jot down a message to a friend or relative, accidently using nursing shorthand, and then they ask you what a 'c' with a horizontal line over it means?"

–Linda Hazlett, RN
Bedford, Virginia

"...Before retiring for the night, your clothes are laid out neatly, much like those of a firefighter preparing for an emergency. You're on call."

–Holly Klinger, RN, CNOR
Brecksville, Ohio

"…You are in a parking lot, feel a yank on your shoulder from behind, can only think that someone is falling and you are going to turn around quickly to help them, only to expose your purse and have it pulled from your shoulder and stolen."

–Elizabeth Mauncele, MSN, BS, RN, CCM
Gettysburg, Pennsylvania

"…You run into someone out in public who hails you down to thank you for taking 'such good care' of them, but you don't recognize them with their clothes on!"

–Kenneth C. Montgomery
Pottsville, Pennsylvania

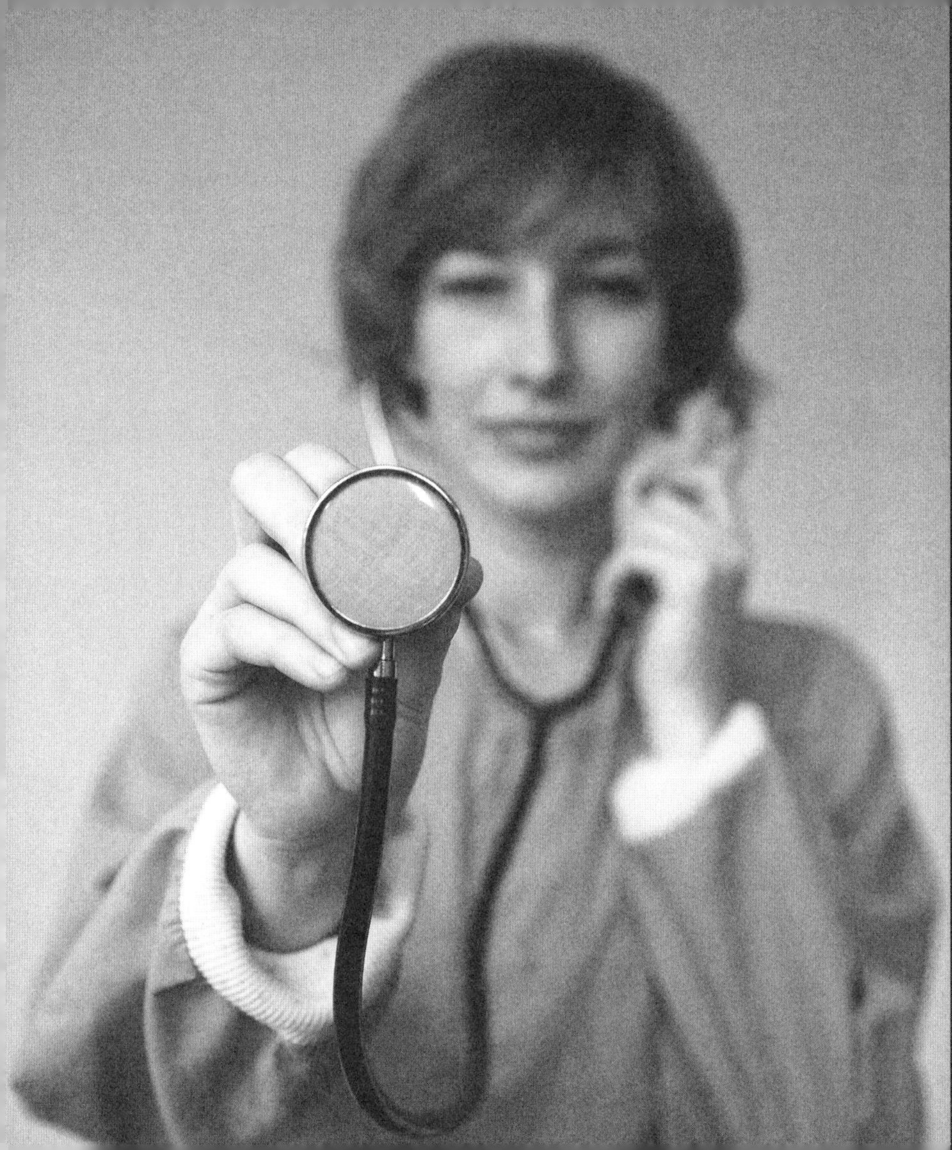

"…You have put RN behind your name so often that you sign it on a personal cheque."

–Kathryn Rousseau, MScN
Windsor, Ontario, Canada

"…You're home from work, sick, and you're worried about your patients, and call in to check on them."

–Judy A. Wessell, RN, NP
Virginia Beach, Virginia

"…You're at the local mall in street clothes and a former patient recognizes you and thanks you for the great care."

–Doris Cavlovich, RN, MSN
Pittsburgh, Pennsylvania

5

assessing

you'll know you're a nurse when …

"…You look at people's feet, and shoe choice, and imagine what services they'll need in the future."

–Marilyn Webster, RN, MSN
Galloway, Ohio

"…You start triaging your family's Christmas celebrations and your neighbor brings both their kids and pets for care."

–Pam Willson, PhD, RN, FNP, BC
Houston, Texas

"…Your neighbors knock on your door to describe their own, their spouse's, and their children's medical ailments in hopes of your expert nursing advice."

–Jason Powell, RN, BScN, MScN, CEN
Toronto, Ontario, Canada

"…You are able to formulate a tentative care plan for the person ahead of you in line at the supermarket."

–Renee A. Prechtl, BSN, RN
Bemus Point, New York

"...While attending the local art museum, you 'diagnose' all illnesses portrayed in the human subjects in the paintings."

–Peggy Doyle, MS, RN
Centerville, Ohio

"…All of your relatives and most of your friends consider you their primary medical person for information and advice."

–Gerri Kucharik, RN, MS, CHPN
Palm City, Florida

"…With just one look at a person, and within a couple of seconds, you've gone through at least three different diagnoses."

–Davey Voss, BSN, RN
Mendon, Illinois

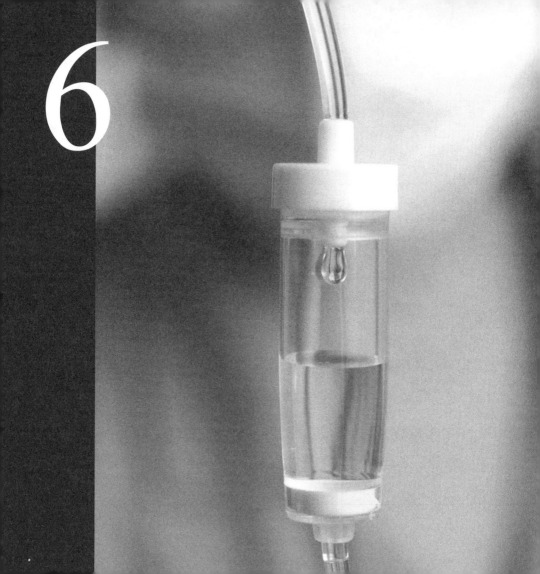

6

veins

"…You go to the gym, look at a nice set of biceps, and think 'what a great vein for an IV.'"

–Dolores Greenwood, RN, MSN
Los Angeles, California

"…You are standing in line somewhere, see another person's hand, and think 'Yes, I could get an 18 in there—no problem.'"

–Robin Hertel
Hays, Kansas

"…You find yourself 'drooling' over a gentleman's large veins as you ride the elevator."

–Cheryl Rowder, RN, PhD, CCRC
Georgetown, Texas

"…You're sitting on a bus next to a really gorgeous guy, and you think to yourself, 'Wow, he's got really good veins!'"

–*Cheryl Hoyt Zambroski, RN, PhD*
Tampa, Florida

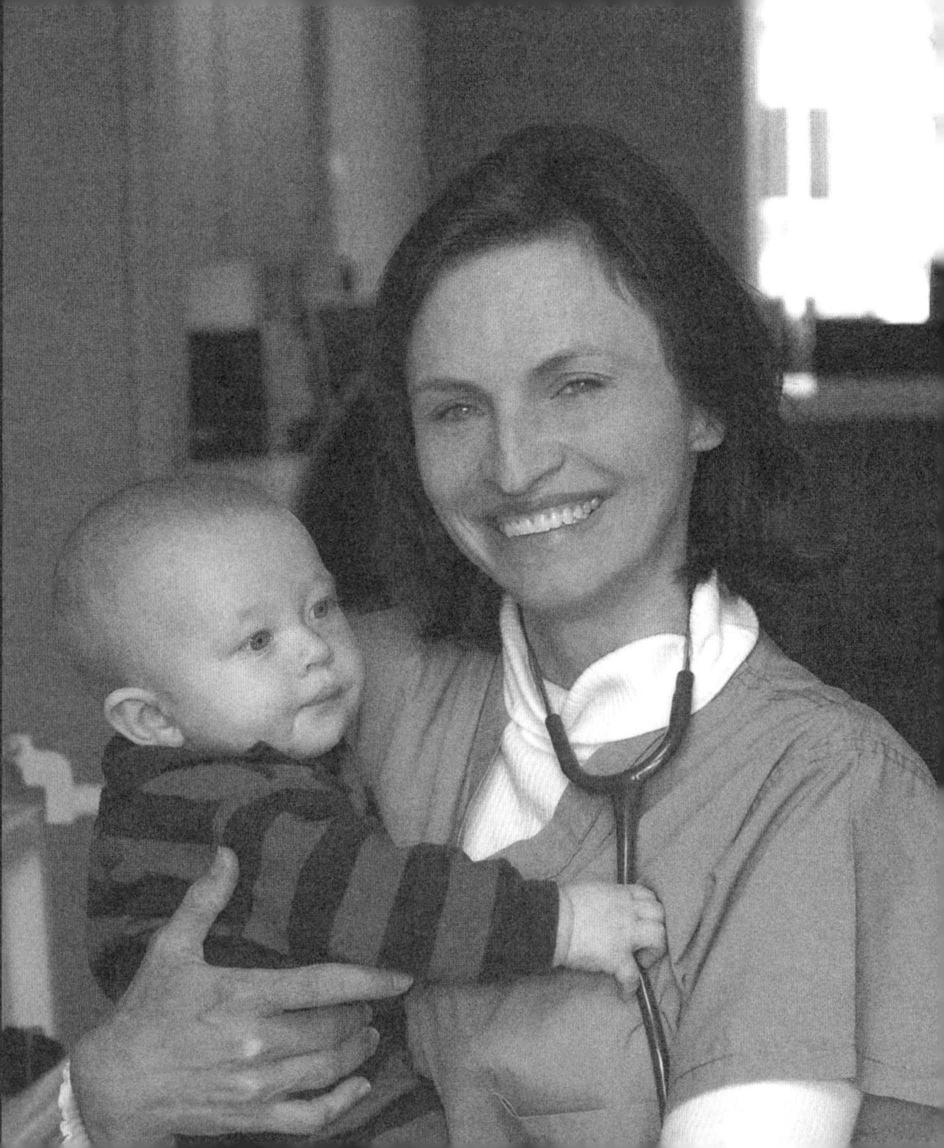

"…You reach over to touch your husband's hand tenderly in the middle of the night and find yourself feeling for a vein."

–Amy Zavesky, RN, BSN
Lansing, Illinois

"…You are standing in line looking at people's veins thinking, 'Ooh . . . that's a good one!'"

–Amy Oliver, RN, BSN
Austin, Texas

"…You realize that the medical student you taught to insert an IV is now an attending physician."

–Sherry Fox, RN, PhD, CNRN
Chesterfield, Virginia

"…Your husband's eyes lovingly acknowledge that you're staring at his veins again."

–Renee Fowler, RN, BSN
Seattle, Washington

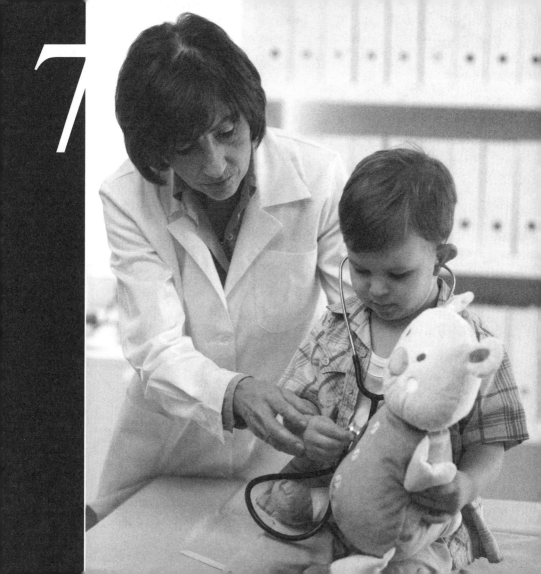

7

patients

"…Your patient tells you that the things you did for him and taught him were invaluable; that he appreciates your compassion and passion for the art of nursing."

–*Glenda Schaffer, RSN, CMS, RN*
Hays, Kansas

"…A sweet elderly lady looks at you, smiles, and whispers 'thank you, dear,' and your heart soars.

–Marilyn Sutton, BScN, MA
Amherstburg, Ontario, Canada

"…Your patient load includes a patient who dies, a patient who awakens from a coma, a patient who decides to discontinue treatment, and a patient who is discharged."

–Sandra W. Haak, PhD, APRN
Sandy, Utah

"...You're able to describe a patient care situation in which you advocated on a patient's behalf, and, on reflection, you knew it was because the patient's interest was served."

–Frostenia Milner, MSN, RN, CNA, LNC
Greensboro, North Carolina

A colleague working at a public health clinic told of a patient who had had multiple children that were conceived prior to the woman's six-week follow-up for the most recent newborn. After the birth of her latest child, she asked for help with contraception, so the staff taught her how to use a diaphragm. They told her in order to avoid 'slip ups' just insert it every night in case she and her husband were intimate. She indicated she understood, and the nurses thought they had done a great job of teaching. Six weeks later at her follow up, her pregnancy test was positive. The staff was dumfounded. She assured them she was inserting the diaphragm every night. Further assessment revealed the patient's husband worked nights and was home during the day, underscoring the importance of a thorough history and very careful word selection.

–Jeanie Burt, MSN, MA, RN, CNE
Searcy, Arkansas

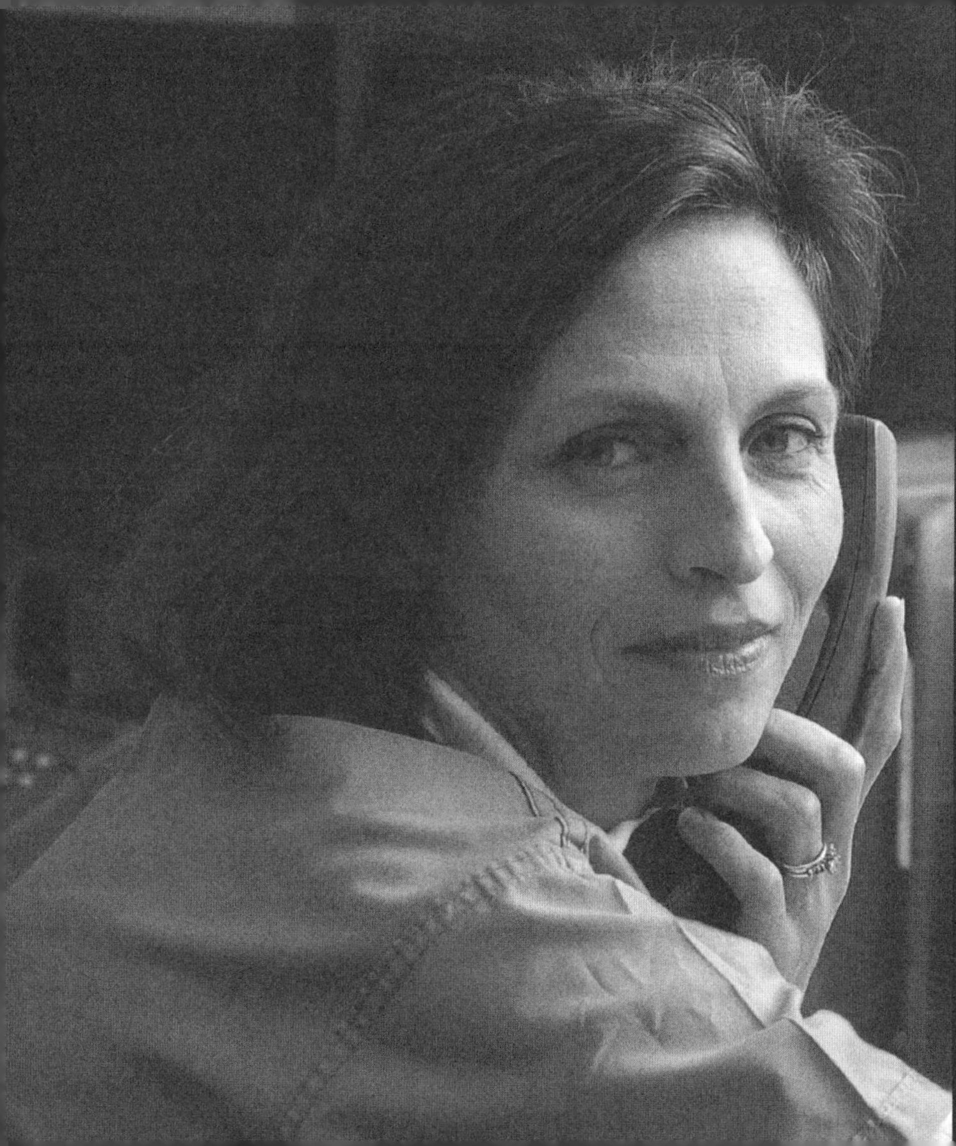

"…Your coworkers run into your patient's room with the crash cart while you're bathing that patient in bed and having a conversation with her. Your coworkers say, 'She is in asystole,' and you're able to turn and say 'No, she's receiving a bath.'"

–Glenda Schaffer, RSN, CMS, RN
Hays, Kansas

"…A patient's family member calls you at home to let you know her father has died."

–Pam Willson, PhD, RN, FNP, BC
Houston, Texas

"…You have successfully completed a shift in which you started four IVs on four new pediatric admits, participated in two codes (one good outcome and one bad outcome), completed your documentation, and are excited about repeating it tomorrow!"

–*Cathy Northrup, RN, MSN, CPN*
Abilene, Texas

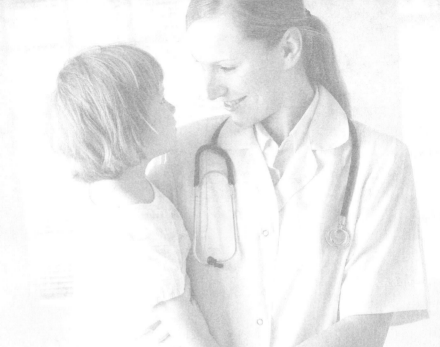

"…You're the only one on rounds who knows the name of a child's imaginary friend and that the intern is about to sit on him."

–Martha Driessnack, RN, PhD
Des Moines, Iowa

"…Your 97-year-old, teary-eyed patient says, 'My journey has about ended' and you tear up, take time, and stay for a while."

–Alma Sullivan, BSN, RN, LNC
Vicksburg, Mississippi

"…You care for a family whose beliefs directly conflict with yours and treat them as you would your own family."

–Christine Narad, APRN, BC
Oakton, Virginia

"…A patient states that you saved his life and, if it wasn't for you, he wouldn't be here today."

–Connie K. Cupples, RN, MS, MSN
Bartlett, Tennessee

"…You just comforted a dying patient and his or her family, and then continued on to your next patient with a smile and encouraging words."

–Linda Crawford, RN, BSN, NCSN
Barre, Massachusetts

"…You haven't forgotten an AIDS patient. He and family braved closed, ice-covered roads to give you a red rose and a kiss at work—a forever goodbye."

–Joan Bailey-Enderson, RN, BSN
Plattsmouth, Nebraska

"…A family member of a deceased patient sees you in the grocery store and comes up to you, hugs you, and says 'I will never forget your kindness to our mother.'"

–Cynthia Moore
Camden, Delaware

"…A patient calls you to his room and reaches for your hand before he'll let the physician give him the results of the tumor biopsy."

–Robin Easley, MNSc, RN
Little Rock, Arkansas

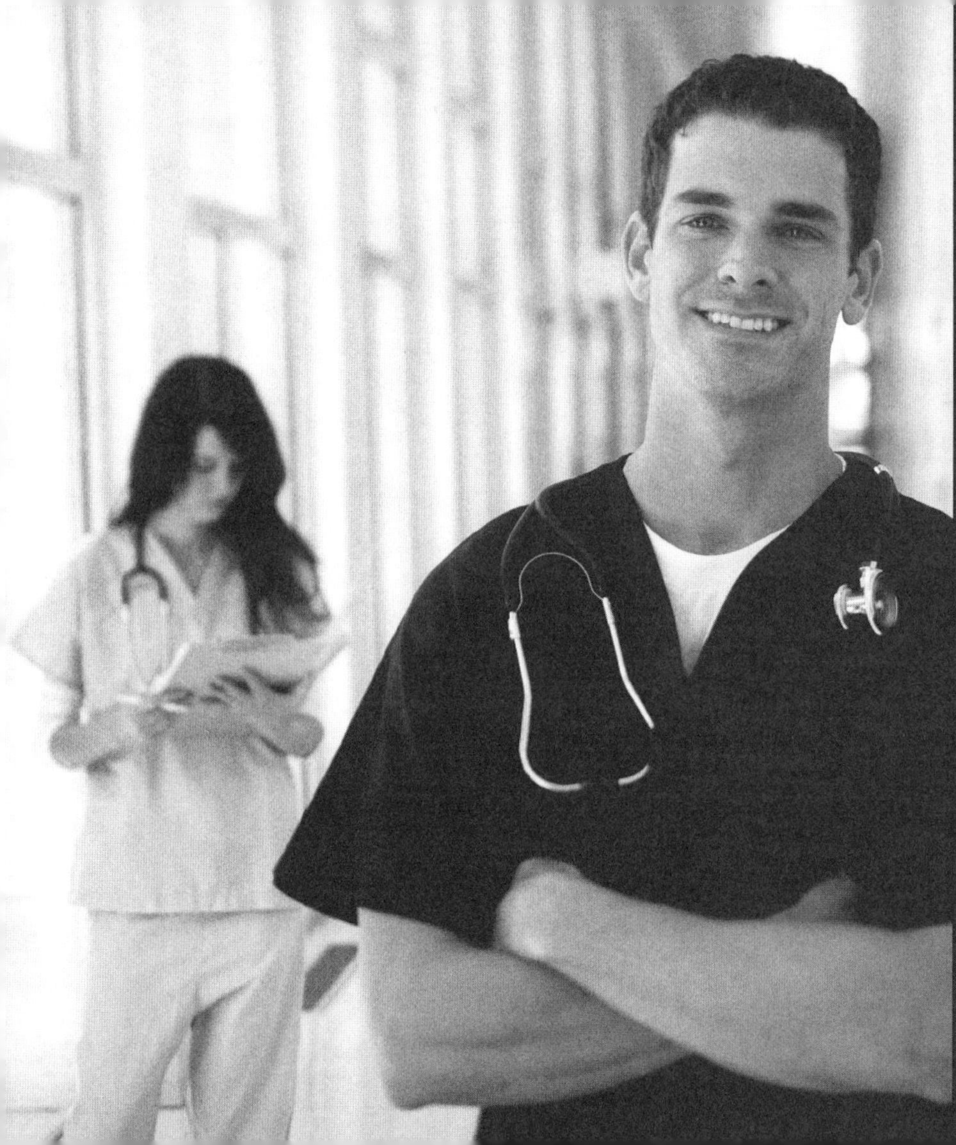

77 patients

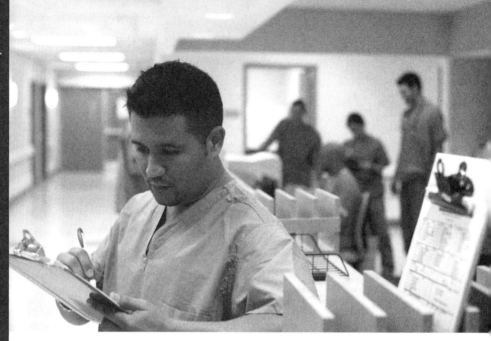

"…You write times of medication administration on the bed sheet during a code."

—Marlienne Goldin, RN, BSN, MPA
Greensboro, North Carolina

"…A patient tells you, 'Oh! Your smile makes me feel better already, I don't need the doctor or medicine.'"

–*Usha K. Gaji, RN, PHN, BSN, MSN/ED*
Yuba City, California

Doing foot care required patients to pre-soak for 10 minutes. One summer morning, a 72-year-old gentleman wearing shorts and rubber boots was waiting for foot care. 'No,' he said, 'I can't soak my feet, I have things to do.' At that point, he pulled his feet out of his rubber boots. He had been up since 5 a.m., had filled his rubber boots with water and wore them while he worked in his garden and had coffee with his buddies at a nearby restaurant . . . It was now 9 a.m. He had the cleanest, most shriveled feet I had ever seen!

–*Rosanna Gartley, RN, CRNP, PBG*
McKees Rocks, Pennsylvania

As a nursing professor, I do nursing through students. A new acquaintance who found this out asked me if I could still be a nurse, and, if so, could I do nursing on a mission trip? These questions led to reflection, new adventures, and a five-year relationship with a little boy I met at a makeshift hospital in rural Guatemala. I met Ebilio when he was a month old with a bilateral cleft lip and palate. Through these trips, I reconnected with the reasons I had became a nurse and watched Ebilio's life change as, first his lip, then his palate, and, finally two fistulas were repaired. I am also able now to include students in the trips, showing them a different side of nursing.

–Karen Eberle, MSN, RNC-OB, CNE
Sioux City, Iowa

'Jane,' a developmentally disabled woman presented for HIV pretest counseling, having received blood transfusions for postpartum hemorrhaging. Not comprehending her positive diagnosis, she walked out and resumed her life.

Over the next few years I educated Jane about HIV and encouraged treatment compliance. As she became cognizant of her approaching death, she said: 'I would like to be buried with my father so I won't be alone when I die, but I don't know where he is.'

Through an historian, we located her father's interment site. Jane was buried next to him after her long battle with AIDS.

Jane's bravery and the lessons she taught me about dealing with illness, life, and death, continue to impact my practice to this day.

–Maria Taylor, CNS, FNP-BC
Valhalla, New York

End of life is difficult, especially when working in pediatrics. It isn't just about taking care of the patient because taking care of the parent is just as important. Sue stayed at her son's side 24 hours a day. She was tired, moody, and worn out. Max was 13, a DNR, and facing the end of his life. She refused to leave his side. After three months of caring for him, I convinced Sue to go home and celebrate her daughter's 10th birthday. Two hours after she left, he coded and passed away without her there. I was terrified to face her. How could I let her son die without her? Later, after an emotional goodbye, Sue yelled out for me, held out her arms, and embraced me. She looked right in my eyes and said 'thank you.' It was a moment I will never forget.

–Melissa Hernandez, RN, BS, BSN
Whittier, California

"…You get an appreciation note from family members or the patient, and you get all emotional and cry with them."

–Usha K. Gaji, RN, PHN, BSN, MSN/ED
Yuba City, California

I worked on a cardiac floor as a new BSN graduate. An elderly lady had I worked on a cardiac floor as a new BSN graduate. An elderly lady had such profound end-stage congestive heart failure that you could hear her death rattle well outside her room. I questioned her untouched breakfast that morning, and she responded with a feeble, faltering whisper: 'May I please have biscuits and gravy?' Her countenance fell when the physician told her that it would be too much salt for her. Later, I asked the physician if we could get her some biscuits and gravy as she was near death and perhaps it would bring her some joy. The next morning she had biscuits and gravy. She ate just a few bites, but I have never seen such a beautiful smile as she mouthed 'thank you.' She died peacefully the next day.

–Jeanie Burt, MSN, MA, RN, CNE
Searcy, Arkansas

"…You embrace a grieving family, and your tears mingle with theirs."

–Marlienne Goldin, RN, BSN, MPA
Greensboro, North Carolina

"…After 17 years of advance practice, you can give your dying mother a pristine bed bath you learned in 1960 in Nursing 101."

–Virginia Wheeler
Sunnyside, Utah

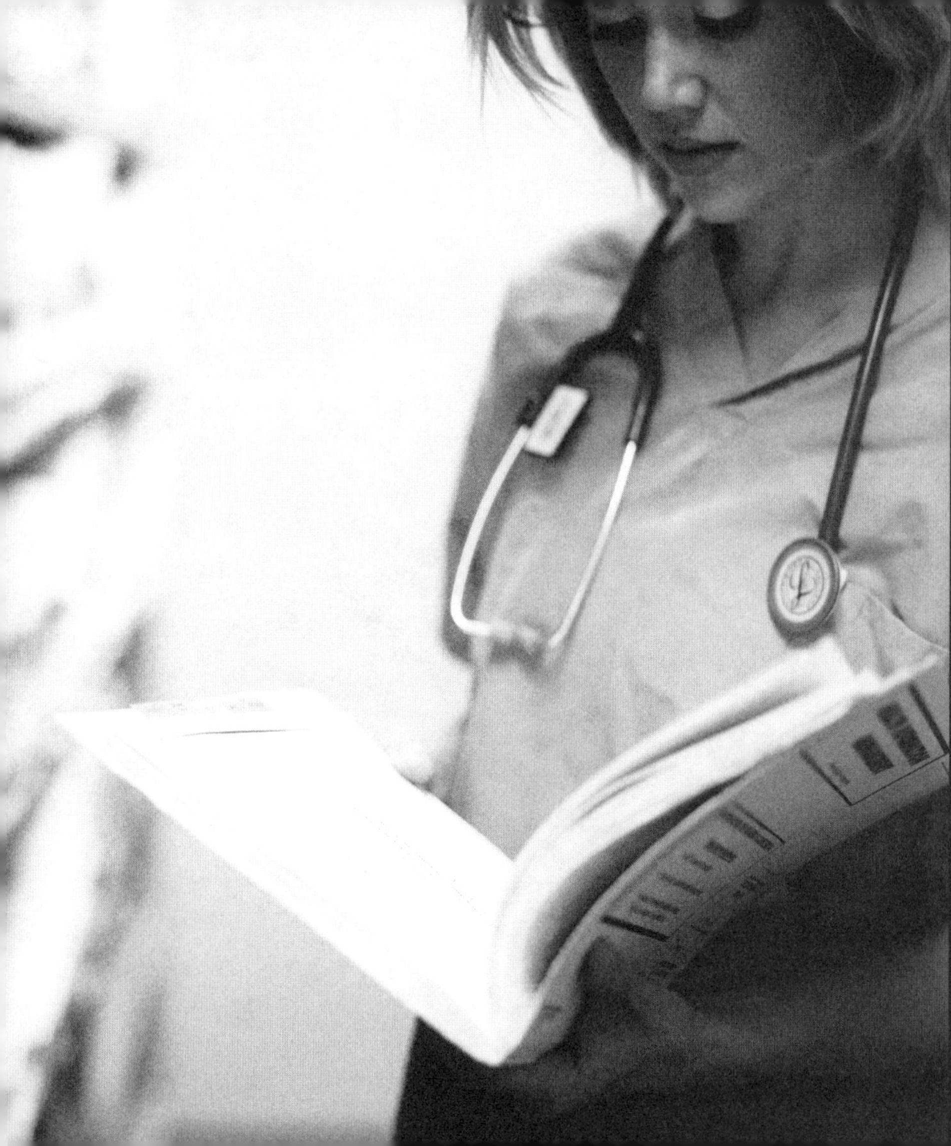

87 patients

Index of Authors

Experience Membership!

Honor Society of Nursing, Sigma Theta Tau International membership provides tools and resources to meet your specific needs at every turn in your career, including:

Access to FREE Continuing Nursing Education
Take advantage of more than 36 hours of professional development. Courses rotate on a regular basis.

Online Networking Opportunities
Join member-driven Facebook and LinkedIn groups. Or, check out the member forums.

Reflections on Nursing Leadership **Member-only e-magazine**
Read *RNL* today! Fresh stories and content updates are added virtually every day.

Member-only Discount
Visit Nursing Knowledge International, www.nursingknowledge.org, and receive 10% off books and continuing nursing education published by STTI.

www.nursingsociety.org/membership

Sigma Theta Tau International
Honor Society of Nursing

Complete listing of member benefits available online.